The Art Of Worship: Drawing Near To God

Craig A Morrisey

Copyright © 2017 Craig Morrisey

All rights reserved.

ISBN:0692905448
ISBN-13:978-0692905449

Acknowledgments

I thank God for this opportunity to write from my heart to help people strengthen their relationship and worship toward the Lord. I realize that without His anointing and guidance, I wouldn't be where I am today. I am thankful and humbled for the gifts and talents He has blessed me with. It's a privilege and an honor to be used by God, for His Glory, to help people. I would like to thank my Beautiful wife Crystal Morrisey. Thanks for believing in me and pushing me through the rough times where I couldn't see or hear what God was saying in my life. Thank you for trusting me to lead our family and pointing us in the right direction as the Lord leads me. You have been instrumental in my life changing and growing over these last 12 years. For that, I love you from the bottom of my heart. I couldn't think of anyone else I would want to spend the rest of my life with. I would like to thank my mom and my dad. What you have taught me over the years will never be forgotten. I will cherish your love and guidance for the rest of my life. I would like to thank my spiritual father in the Lord, Bishop Donald Crooms Sr. Looking over my life, these last fourteen years, I can see the decision I made to follow you in ministry has been paramount to my growth in the Lord and as a man. Thank you for pushing me and allowing me to see there was more in me than I knew myself. To my family and my church family, Thank You! Thank you for your continuing love and support over the years. For the people like Mrs. Danah Wright and others that help me edit and prepare this manuscript so the world could see and read it, THANK YOU! I am very grateful for your help and this couldn't be possible without you.

DEDICATION

This book is dedicated to everyone who desires a closer walk with God. To the people who desire to make God the center of their lives and live a life of Worship towards Him.

CONTENTS

	Introduction	i
1	You Are Welcome	Pg 1
2	You Deserve It	Pg 10
3	Living A Life For God	Pg 16
4	Worship Initiates Victory	Pg 25
5	Worship Brings Change	Pg 35
6	Worship Is Not A Chore	Pg 43
7	Worship Reveals Your Heart	Pg 51
8	Worship Produces Love	Pg 61
9	When We Worship, We Allow God To Amaze Us	Pg 71
10	I'm Determined To Worship And Live For God	Pg 84

Introduction

Often times when it comes to discussing the topic of worship toward our Lord and Savior Jesus Christ and our Heavenly Father, we leave some minor details out. We perceive the only way to worship God is in church setting or when we are home alone in a quiet place. We have read the scripture in John 4:24 that states **"*God is a Spirit and they that worship him must worship him in spirit and truth"*.** This is true. When we get to that place where we are reverencing God in a intimate setting, when it's just Him and I, that is a must.

When we dedicate that alone time from everything else in this world, we need to tap into that place were we put everything aside and focus solely on our Father. We can't allow distractions of the world, our flesh, family or anything else to take our attention away from Christ. Truth is told, when we enter that intimate place with God, it's not about us anymore. When we praise God, we are thankful for Him being God foremost, and all the things He has done for us. If we are part of a charismatic culture, we may shout with our mouths or we may dance with our feet as David danced. Our thankfulness to God sometimes causes us to run or exuberate praise; but when it comes to worship, a select few becomes bored.

When we worship, it doesn't matter how we feel or what's going on around us. Praise makes us feel good. We feel like we are actually doing something constructive with our limbs as far as dancing and running. Often times when we enter into worship, things slow down. It's not about our step any more. It's about our Father in Heaven and Him alone. Our feelings are lost in the shuffle, because at that moment, all we care about is pleasing our Father. That's that intimate worship that John was talking about.

Merriam-Webster defines Worship as a reverence offered to a divine being or supernatural power; also an act of expressing such reverence. **Merriam-Webster** also defines Reverence as an honor or respect felt or shown; profound adoring awed respect. So we see, worship to our Heavenly Father goes beyond that quiet place and time with Him one on one. Our lives should be a daily reminder to the world how much we worship our father. The way we live and carry ourselves should be an indicator to someone when they see us that something is different about us. Worship doesn't stop after we leave our church settings, as we like to call it, the four walls.

The bible tells us that we are the church. In 1 Corinthians 12:27 it states, **"Now you are the body of Christ and each one of you is a part of it".** Our worship is not limited to the building. When we leave the building, the world needs to see Christ in us. Living a life of constant worship toward God allows us to show it. We must Reverence God in every way possible.

That is why I wanted to write this book. I wanted to give some devotionals that we could read daily or read all at once. To show us how worship should be the way we live and not just something we do every now and then. I wanted us to understand that it's just not a lifestyle change or fad that we switch back and forth on. Like we do when we take part in a diet. We try it for a while and then we switch back to what we where comfortable eating. No, I want this to become who we are. I want us to realize that living a life in reverence to God is not an astronomical feat that we can't accomplish. God has sent us a helper in this world name the Holy Spirit and He is willing to help us if we want it.

My prayer is, after you read these devotionals, you will understand how to go after God's heart. Understand how to get closer to God and how our lives should mirror God in every way possible. So that people all over the world want to have what we have. My prayer is, we never cease worshipping God. Remember, worship doesn't stop after a quiet intimate setting with God. Our daily walk of life should be a constant worship to Him, our Father!

You Are Welcome

"O God, thou art my God, early will I seek thee: my soul thirst for thee"- Psalm 63:1

Life has a way of speeding up time and causing us to feel rushed or pressured. We have many responsibilities in life i.e. taking care of the family, jobs, school, careers and etc. Everyday becomes a grind and we find ourselves starting a daily routine to keep some sense of stability or timing to our day. We figure that if we stay on our routine that everything will work out the way it needs to be. God forbid something happens to us throughout the day or to knock our routine out of whack, we feel lost or discombobulated. Sometimes it's hard for us to gather ourselves when things get out of line and doesn't go according to schedule.

I would like to pose a question. How often do we welcome God in our lives every morning? How often do wake up and go straight into our daily routine? I know we all have busy lives and we set our alarm clocks so that when we get up, we know exactly how much time we have before we have to be to work, school or etc. We have it mapped out but how often do we wake up and before we check emails, social media or grab our morning coffee, we tell God good morning? How often do you welcome God into your day? How often do we give Him permission to do as He pleases with our day, no matter our schedule or routine? These are questions that we need to ask ourselves, because I want to present to you a case that by welcoming God into our lives when we wake up and giving Him permission to lead us throughout the day is the first step to understanding, submitting and going after God's Heart.

David tells God in Psalms 63:1 " Oh God thou art my God, early will I seek thee: my soul thirst for thee, my flesh long for thee in a dry and thirsty land". David let it be known to God that as I rise this morning, the first thing I want to do is to seek you. David realized that without God, his day would feel empty or void. David understood that if he started his day acknowledging and welcoming the father into his day that whatever he needed in that day would be fulfilled. Sometimes we feel as if it would take to much time to pray to God or spend time with God because we need our sleep in the morning or our routine will not allow time. I believe David knew that his daily routine had to start with welcoming God into his heart and space. He recognized that starting your day off with God gave strength, power, joy and a fulfillment that couldn't be described. David decreed that " Because thy loving kindness is better than life and my lips shall praise thee" Psalms 63:3. He knew if it hadn't been for God, life, as he knew it wouldn't exist. We have to see everyday the same. It sounds so simple yet we often by pass God in the morning and catch up with Him sometime throughout the day.

    I want to challenge us to start our day off with God. No matter what state of mind we may be in, God is always waiting to hear from us. God takes pleasure in knowing no matter how busy our day may be, the first thing we want to do as we arise to start the day is to welcome Him and allow Him to have his way in our life. It's something about meeting God early in the morning. That life connection that we make as soon as we wake up gives us the strength to face any and everything that comes our way throughout the day. David said I am satisfied from my encounter with God every morning. His soul long for God in a way that nothing but God's presence could fill that void. Do we long for God in that way when we open our eyes in the morning? Do we really grasp that God is our source and our strength? Do we realize that His love and kindness and better than anything that we can encounter?

When was the last time that you gave God permission to have his way in life? I want us to start asking ourselves these questions to bring our lives back in line with the will and heart of God. Because I believe God has missed us and He longs for us to get back to our first love. Do you remember when we first started living this life with Christ, we were so eager to talk with God. We felt incomplete if we didn't start our day our talking to Him and loving on Him. We felt like David, "Thy Love and kindness is better than life so my lips shall praise thee". We didn't see it as a chore or being forced to worship God in the morning. We knew that was our lifeline that we needed in order for our day to go according to plan. Knowing that if something came to deter us, that it didn't matter because all things work together for our good Romans 8:28.

As we continue to grow up and life becomes more chaotic and hectic, we begin to put other things in that space where we used to allow God reside. God wants us to get back to that place that were we needed Him and realized that if we didn't have Him, we couldn't function properly.

Therefore, as you are reading this, I want us to align ourselves back up with the will and heart of God. I want us to realize how much God has missed our one-on-one time in the morning and throughout the day. He is waiting on us the same way we used to meet Him.

How would you feel if you had to meet someone for a business meeting or a scheduled appointment but every time you showed up to the meeting the other person never came? I believe we would grow tiresome of being stood up. We would start to feel like the person doesn't have any interest in us, or the person was wasting our time. Well, how do you think God feels when he shows up to meet us and we are not there? God is not like us, He will keep showing up everyday just in case you decide to show up and have our normal talks.

Therefore, I encourage us to get back to seeking God and welcoming Him into our lives as we arise in the morning. I believe that our lives will start to be satisfied and fulfilled to the place where nothing bothers us or throws us off our game. I want to pray a prayer with you

"Lord, I want to thank You for Your love and kindness You have shown toward me. I want to tell You that I'm sorry for not starting my day off with You like I should have. I'm sorry that I have let life cause me to fill rushed and that I don't have enough time in my busy schedule for You. On this day, I pledge my love, time and my heart back to You. Regardless of my circumstances Father, You are welcome in my life and I give You permission to have Your way. I love You with

my whole heart in Jesus name

Amen".

You Deserve It

"With All my heart, I will Glorify your name forevermore"-Psalm 86:12

I woke up one morning and I asked myself a question. Are we really thankful and grateful for the life that God has given us? Do we take God for granted? Do we allow our minds to comprehend all that God has allowed to happen? How He allowed His only Son to die for us in order to allow us to worship Him in spirit and in truth? I know our lives may not be perfect and we may not have everything that we want or feel we need sometimes; however, God is still worthy of all the praise and our worship towards Him.

I have learned in life, we have to find something to be grateful for. Its not that we don't have problems or different obstacles we face everyday, but it is the acknowledgement to God that in spite of our life challenges, we choose to be grateful. Being grateful has to be a state of mind. As individuals, we need the state of mind that we are because of Him. Once we are thankful, our thankfulness will turn into adoration towards our Lord and savior.

In the bible, my adoration for David was he always made reference to God in a state of worship. No matter what situation he found himself in; whether he was under attack or if he was living a life of riches, he always realized that everything he had accomplished, it was because of God. Are we using David as an example of having a heart after God or do we allow our life's challenges to overrule our worship towards God? I found out that as long as we live, there will always be some complaint or anger. I feel David could have complained about a lot of things in his life; but he always found a way to bring it back to God with his worship and his thankfulness.

I believe that what we need to start doing this in our lives today. We need to find a way to turn every situation into worship unto the Lord. Let me give you an example; I was dealing with a situation and I couldn't understand why it seemed as if every time I thought I was moving forward in life, I would began to stall. I will not lie to you, I got frustrated and wanted to quit. At that moment, I wasn't seeing the "good" in that situation to allow me to worship God or be grateful. I couldn't see how to be thankful because I was allowing my situation to dictate my attitude.

My attitude was tied to my gratefulness. My gratefulness was tied to my heart. My heart was supposed to be tied to my worship unto the Lord but I allowed my heart, my disappointments and struggle to dictate my response to God. How did it dictate my response to God? I walked around living but not full of life. I couldn't see God's goodness because of my attitude. It wasn't until I changed my attitude and decided to worship God in spite of everything that I received my answer to what I was seeking.

I had a "light bulb" moment in my mind. I

realized that my circumstances do not dictate my worship but my worship to God changes how I see my situation. We have to realize that when we worship God, it's not for us. Our worship to God should not be contingent upon how we feel or if we have life all together. Our worship must come from our love towards God, knowing that in spite of all our mess ups. God still loves us. Even when God is frustrated with us, He never leaves us or forsakes us. God is always there and for that, worship should always be on our lips and flow from our hearts.

Life should never dictate our worship to God. Our worship toward God should always dictate our lives. When we can live a life of worship that way, we honor God in everything that we do. Lets pray this prayer together

"Lord we love You and thank You for being God in our

lives. We want to tell You on this day that we are sorry for allowing our circumstances and life challenges to dictate our worship towards You. We want to say we are sorry for not always acknowledging Your goodness towards us, even when we don't understand our obstacle that we face. From this day forward, we dedicate our lives to You. We will worship You with our whole hearts. Our lives will become a testament to Your goodness and mercy towards us. With your help God, we will forever be grateful and allow our walk to become a constant worship towards You, in Jesus name

Amen".

Living A Life For God

"Whatever you do, work at it wholeheartedly as though you were doing it for the Lord and not merely for people"-Colossians 3:23

Have you ever read something and it changed your outlook on life? If you are reading a good book, maybe a self-help book and it gives you a WOW moment that changes your perspective of things. This is how I fell when I read this particular scripture in Colossians. I had to ask myself a simple but powerful question. "Am I living my life to please God or to please people? Am I doing everything unto God in my life or am I just trying to scape by?"

The scripture continues to say, *"**knowing with all certainty that it is from the Lord not men that you will receive the inheritance, which is your greatest reward. It is the Lord Christ whom we actually serve**"*. I question myself, do we actually live our lives like that? Our worship to God doesn't stop after we spend time with God in our secret and quite places. Our worship continues even when we leave our homes for work, school, etc. Everything we do in life is a reflection of how we see and reverence God.

Do you understand we have to change our mindset and pray to God everyday we become what this world needs to see when they look at us? Trust me, I know it is hard to accomplish everyday. I understand how your supervisor may frustrate you and the thought comes to mind get away to the back to coast today, or if you are in school and you're feeling the teacher is "pushing" you, therefore, you shut down for the day; or when you are driving and a car cuts in front of you after a long exhausting day, how do you act?

Do you remember everything we do is an indicator to God that you want your life to reflect your love towards Him? Our worship towards God changes how we see life. Colossians 3:23 says that everything we do, work at it wholeheartedly as if we are working for God. I believe this scripture is really explanatory. Do we really live our lives like that? Do we make sure that when we find ourselves slacking that we pick ourselves up because our lives are really not our own?

We have been commissioned to live our lives unto God. Now I will be honest with you, I have to check myself daily. I'm one that if not careful, to let procrastination creep in and make me stagnant in certain areas of my life. It causes me to not be as sharp as I need to be for that day. Procrastination causes us to become lackadaisical in our thinking and causes us to not give our all every time. We put stuff off for a while and say we will come back to it. If we are honest with ourselves, usually we never get back to it. If we are not careful, procrastination becomes a state of being for us. It becomes our culture and when that happens, we are not living a life towards God. We become stagnant and never get things accomplished.

By now you are reading this and saying what does this have to do with worship unto God. As I mentioned, worship is not just you alone with God in your quite place or alone time. Worship is how you live your life towards God. Our life signifies our worship to God by how we honor the very life He breathes into our bodies every morning. It's our responsibilities to make sure we are careful how we live our lives and we are making an impact for God on this earth. Everyday we should see it as an opportunity to lead by example. If we can show the world how to live a life unto God, it would be in a better place.

You may ask, "how do we accomplish such feats"? By becoming the examples that God wanted to see in the earth in the first place. Whether you are in the stock market, cashier, teacher, banker, or a trash collector, Do it unto God. That's the type of worship unto God that is missing in the world today. We have stopped loving the process of life and we short-change everything. When we live this way, we are not showing God that we care or love His ways towards us. Everyday our lives should constantly remind people of how awesome our God is. Our upbeat attitude and attention to details should make people question, how are they working so hard or how are they accomplishing so much in life? Our work ethic in life should be a direct reflection of God's goodness, love, mercy, and favor towards us. When God sees us, it should make him proud to call us sons and daughters. Our lifestyle should become our daily worship unto God.

Everything we do should show God we are appreciative for our life, health and strength. Our life should become a constant reminder to everyone that we honor God by the way we live. In other words, when we feel like slacking, we should not, because that wouldn't honor God. When we feel like quitting, we find strength in God to continue to fight through it. Understanding this is how we honor God and live a life unto Him.

We have to change our outlook on life and see it the way that God sees it. We have to pray to God to allow us to see life through his eyes. When we see things His way, we have the opportunity to show others how to persevere through hardships and difficult tasks in our everyday lives. Therefore, when different challenges present themselves on our jobs, school or in our lives, let us ask ourselves a simple question. If we quit here, would our lives please God? What type of example would we show the world if we allow everything to stop us from finishing the task at hand?

By finishing our assignments in life, it becomes our worship to God. When others see our worship, it causes them to inquire to us, "how do we do it"? How are we able to not let things hinder us from accomplishing our assignments in life? At that moment we have an opportunity to share where our strength comes from. We are able to tell them about our <u>Lord and Savior Jesus Christ</u>. How He gives us strength day by day and how we pledged to live a life of worship towards Him. Lets pray together,

"Father, I love and thank You for Your many blessings You have given us all through life. Today, we come asking You to give us strength to live this life unto You. Help us to do everything wholeheartedly towards You. Let us live a life that is pleasing towards You and that everyday You find joy in breathing life into our bodies. Father let our lives become a constant worship to You in everything we do. We pray to make You happy and honor You with this precious life You have given us

In Jesus name,

***Amen**"*

Worship Initiates Victory

"Come to me, all you who are weary and heavily burdened, and I will give you rest. Take my yoke upon you and learn from me, for I am gentle and humble in heart and you will find rest for your souls"-Matthew 11:28-29

Often times we look at worship as a task or something that is time consuming. I've notice sometimes when I attend different church settings there is a high praise period when everyone is up and participating. Regretfully when the service shifts to worship, when we are ready to get close to God, people pull back. It's as if we are telling God I will praise you because that feels good to me, but when it comes to worship, I'll wait that out. Unknowingly, worship is for God and there are benefits that come with spending intimate time with the Lord. I have always wondered why people have found it so hard to worship God. Now, there is nothing wrong with praise because praising God is what we have been commissioned to do. There is something sweet about spending that time with God. It relieves stress and worry.

The bible tells us in John chapter 4 verse 24 that ***"God is spirit and those who worship Him must worship in spirit and truth"***. I believe when we read this verse it scares some people away. We have a way of telling ourselves that we are not worthy of worshipping God. We allow our past failures and mistakes to stop us from knowing the power of our Lord and Savior through worshipping Him and spending time with Him. One thing I love about God, He has always wanted us to come spend time with Him. No matter our circumstances, mistakes or set backs, He is always yearning for His people to get to know Him.

If we have made mistakes, because of His son, Jesus Christ, we have been given a way of repentance that allows access to our Father. Fortunately, nothing really can stop you from entering that intimate place with God if you really want to. It is so important to know we all have been given total access to God because of His son Jesus Christ. Jesus died for our sins and created a bridge between God and us. Since Jesus's death, burial and resurrection has taken place, our lives have been forever changed. I am setting a stage for you to realize that your mistakes and hang-ups have no power over you. You do not have to live in torment or fear that you cannot approach God. Once you move past that hurdle, there are so many joys to spending time with God.

Spending time with God initiates victory in our lives. When we set time out of our busy schedules and lives, we let God know He is important to us. Secondly, we create discipline in our lives; because it takes discipline to create time and space for our Father. Life can cause a burden to our schedules, time, jobs, etc., but I love spending intimate time with God. I can enter that place of worship, where none of that other stuff matters. That's why God made that plea to us in Matthew 11:28 to **"Come to me, all who are weary and heavily burdened"**.

When we enter into the presence of God, nothing comes with us but us. Our problems, our anxiety, our burdens and our grief are to be dropped off. When we enter the presence of God, He takes those things away from us. Not saying when we are through spending time with God, that we wont have to deal with things; but there is a joy now that wasn't there before.

It is not a bad thing when the bible tells us "***We must worship Him in spirit and in truth***". God is spirit and when we tap into the spirit of God, He gives us a refreshing like never before. It's as if we are going through a spiritual detox. When we detox our bodies, it cleanses us of everything that could cause our bodies harm. So it is in the spirit when we deal with God. God cleanses us of everything that causes us harm when we enter that place of worship. He takes away our stress, burdens and worry.

Another thing I love about God is that while we are there in His presence, as we worship Him, He downloads into our spirit clear instructions to make it throughout our day and lives. If you know anything about God, His instructions always work. In essence, His instructions always lead to victory. Sometimes God hides things in His presence to draw us closer to Him. So we see, as we worship God for himself and him alone, benefits come with it. Every time I have left the presence of God, I have always come away with something that I never knew. God has always been yearning for us daily. We have allowed the cares of this world to keep us away. But if we ever grasp the concept that he wants to take care of us and relieve us of our stress and burdens, our lives will be better.

We saw in 2nd Chronicles chapter 20, Jehoshaphat worshipped the Lord by seeking His face and was given clear instructions on how to win the battle against a combined army. They were given clear instructions that went against the norm. They were told that this battle that was in front of them was not there to fight. That's another thing I love about our Father. He always knows how to take care of His children.

God spoke through Jahaziel to tell them in verse 15 that "***Do not be afraid. Do not lose hope because of this huge army the battle is not yours, it is God's".*** The bible tells us that after Jehoshaphat heard what was said, they all bowed down and worshipped the Lord. And after the finished worshipping, verse 20-21 says that Jehoshaphat gave clear instructions to the people to gather all of the singers to stand in front of the people of God so that they could sing in unison, all together, ***"Praise the Lord, for His mercy endures Forever"***. That one simple phrase was going to give them victory. But those instructions didn't come to Jehoshaphat until after they worshipped the Lord.

You see, while we are in the presence of God, He gives clear instructions that always lead to victory. Jehoshaphat placed singers out in front of them and as the army came against them, God started fighting for them. When God fights for you, Victory is inevitable. Now you may not have to face an army, but maybe you are facing a sickness, stress of life, worry, family problems or etc. The stress of it all is wearing you down and you can't seem to find an answer.

I implore you to spend time with God on today. Allow your Father to refresh you, cleanse you and strengthen you through His Spirit. After your refreshing, don't leave his presence; stay there until you hear the instructions God has for you. Sometimes the instructions seem crazy and outlandish. It really didn't make sense for Jehoshaphat to put singers out in front of them going into battle. They were going up against a real threat. An army that had intentions on killing them, but when you follow the instructions of God, no matter the threat, Victory is Inevitable!

So today I want to pray with you that we release ourselves of our past and everything that hinders us from spending quality alone time with God

"Father, our God, we come to You today, first telling You thank You for Your son Jesus Christ. Because of Him we are able to stand in Your presence and not be ashamed. Because He died on the cross for us, we are

able to ask for forgiveness. Today we make a vow to You that we will make time for You from now on. No matter how busy our lives are, Father You are what's most important to us. Thank You for loving us even when we weren't spending time with You. Today that changes. You will become our first choice all over again. We are falling back in love with our First Love. We love You and thank You in Jesus Name

Amen.

Worship Brings Change

"Now the Lord is that Spirit and where the Spirit of the Lord is, thee is Liberty"-2 Corinthians 3:17

We all have certain people that we love to hang around. Whether it is our best friends, spouse or etc. we make time to be around them. Do you ever notice that when that person walks in our room or our space, it seems as if things liven up. No matter how we were feeling at the time or what we are going through, those friends spirit brings joy to our lives. We can go from sad talking about our troubles to upbeat and talking about what makes us happy in an instance. Its something about our spirits connecting with their spirits that instantly brings peace. It seems as if they know exactly what to say or do to bring calmness to our lives. Our aura changes immediately when the walk in the room.

I want to ask you a question. If our friends, spouse or love ones have that power, what kind of power do you think God has when we invite Him to come into our space? How different would our lives be if we allowed God to invade our space and change our surroundings? Sometimes we can get to dependent on our spouses, loved ones and friends that we forget the one that gives life to us daily. Now there is nothing wrong with spending time with family, friends or your spouse. We should always make time to spend with them. That brings us closer together and allows us to strengthen each other when we need it. We shouldn't spend more time with them than we spend with God.

One thing I'm learning everyday is we must strive to live a balance life. I know it's hard, because I'm still learning to do it myself. It's as if we are looking at a balance scale. You have to put equal amounts of weight on both sides in order for it to balance out right. What I found out is as long as God is on one side and everything else is on the other side, everything seems to balance out in life. God is strong enough and carries enough weight to make sure life doesn't drag us down. Unfortunately, we will never know that unless we spend time with him. We can listen to the preacher preach and sometimes it goes in one ear and right out the other one. When you take time to spend with God on a one on one premise, your life and surroundings change daily. All we want and need is found in God. When we come to that point in life that nothing else will meet our expectations and needs like God, change and balance began to take place in our lives. It moves from just God yearning for us, to us yearning after God. A hunger begins to stir up in us that's only quenched by our Heavenly Father.

Now let me tell you, I love my wife. I mean I really love my wife. She is my world and I am thankful everyday that she came into my world. I know she loves me unconditionally. There is one thing I've found out. Even with all of her love she gives me, I am not complete or empowered if I do not spend time with God. He is my life giver. His spirit gives me a freedom that can't be described. That's what happens when we worship our Heavenly Father. We invite God into our space and change immediately takes place.

You may ask, how is that possible? When we worship God, we give Him free access to come into our lives and our space. When God shows up, everything that's not like God must leave. We create an atmosphere for God when worship. That atmosphere signals to God that we are ready for Him. It tells God at that present time, nothing else matters to us but Him. When God shows up, everything we need follows along with Him.

That's what I love about God. We worship God for him alone, but when God comes to meet us, He brings what we didn't even ask for. Our longing for Him causes him to automatically produce answers for us. God is our Father and He already knows what we are facing in life.

It brings joy to Him when we prioritize Him over our needs. Especially when we tell God, I know I have a need, but at this moment, nothing else matters but my alone time with you. Nothing else will satisfy me right now unless I spend time with You. When we mature to that place in our lives when nothing else matters but Him, life changes for us. We allow God to initiate Change.

The first thing changes in our lives is our mind. Romans 12:2 says ***"And do not be conformed to this world, but be transformed and progressively changed by the renewing of your mind, so that you may prove what the will of God is, that which is good and acceptable and perfect".*** Worship shifts your mind to a new place in God. Also, we see we aren't supposed to worship one time and then we are set for a lifetime. Romans 12:2 tells us that we have to continually renew our minds daily.

The only way that can take place is if we spend time with God. Our attitude shifts and allow us to see things the way God sees them. One thing I found out, even if our situation doesn't change, but how we perceive it and our attitude towards it change, we can face any obstacle that is place in our lives.

So you see, Worshipping God has an awesome effect on our lives. Unfortunately, we'll never know these things unless we spend time with God. If we are always turning to our friends, family, or spouses for quality time before God, we create a void in our lives; and I don't care how much you try to fill that void with other things, it will always be an empty place there until God fills it. Until we realize the affect that worshipping God has on us and our surroundings, we always be searching for something to meet our needs. Fortunately, when we come to the realization that God is the one who balances our lives out and cause us to be changed for the better, living this life doesn't become so strenuous. We realize that we have an agent of change that is always there for us no matter when or where. Lets pray to Him together

"Oh how we love you God. Thank You for always being there for us. Thank You for always being an agent of change for us. Because of Your love for us and attention to details, our lives are always at the for front of Your mind. Because we spend time with You, change is initiated to everything around us. Thank You for loving us past every hurting place we have encountered in our lives. We honor and give You praise, In Jesus Name

Amen".

Worship Is Not A Chore

"Therefore I urge you, brothers and sisters, by the mercies of God, to present your bodies as a living sacrifice, holy and well pleasing to God, which is your rational act of Worship"-Romans 12:1

Most of us, as we were growing up, and even now, were given chores to do. Some things were different for each household. Some were given allowances to do chores, but some of us were told to do something and we better have it done at the appropriate time. We couldn't give an excuse to why it wasn't done or ask what do we get in return for our service; it just had to be done. To our parents, that didn't seem like a hard thing to ask of us. It was something reasonable they were asking. After all they had done for us, it was the least we could do, to complete our chores.

However, I fell victim to not being grateful for what they were providing for me. Instead of being happy to do what they asked, I made the chore feel like a burden instead of a way to show my appreciation for all they have done. I started to hate doing them. I resented the chore to the point that I started to rebel against it and them. I stop seeing it as my reasonable service to them but something that I was forced to do. That made me not want to do it them at all. I would find creative ways to get out of them. I would make up excuses why I couldn't do them. I started spending so much energy on making up excuses that it became exhausting making up excuses.

Does this sound familiar? I believe there are many things that hindered us from spending time worshipping God. One thing is, we are starting to treat it as a chore we are doing for Him. We are becoming that stubborn child that acts as if God should be grateful that we even acknowledge Him. It has become a burden to us to even spend time with God. We have become so complacent with our lives without Him, that when He calls for us, we drag our feet, kick and scream and make excuses why we cant come. We exert so much energy making excuses that it makes us exhausted. If we are not careful, we'll turn our backs on God because of our rebellious state of mind.

This type of behavior infuriates God. Where and when did we become so ungrateful that we forgot all He has done for us? When I didn't do the things that my parents ask me to do, it made them angry! Then that anger turned to hurt, and hurt turned into disappointment. Why you might ask? In my parents mind, all they had done for me, how they provided for me, fed and clothed me, gave me the things I asked for; the least I could do was to fulfill my responsibilities to them.

If I were honest with myself, they shouldn't have to ask me to even help out or clean around the house. I should have taken it upon myself to just do it because of my gratitude towards them. My gratefulness should have made me think that was nothing to do for them because of all they have done for me over the years. My attitude should have shifted to gratitude instead of thinking that's what they should do.

Well if our parents felt that way, how do we think God feels when we act that way towards him? When we can literally look over life and see how he has opened so many doors for us. How he has healed us and turned our lives around. We knew that we were in a messed up state of mind and God came in a change everything about us. He keeps us and provides for us daily, even when we don't acknowledge or thank him for it. Consequently, we feel He better be grateful when we come to worship him.

I believe God allows us to have epiphanies. He allows things to hit our lives just so we can realize it is because of him we are where we are in life. I've had to learn the hard way in my past. It wasn't until I lost things that I thought were special to me, I realized I was allowing those things to pull me away from God. I got what I wanted and became ungrateful. I became more enamored with the gifts than the gift giver. I forgot to show my appreciation to God. He allowed what I loved the most to be taken away. In the process of God getting my attention, it was then I realized the error of my ways. I believe it hurt God more than it hurt me.

    You may ask, why do I say that? I believe it hurt and disappointed God, because he had to allow all that to happen just to get my attention. At the end of the day, all God wants is to know that we are grateful for his many blessings. Our gratefulness is what causes us to worship him. The very thought of his presence causes us to give him spontaneous worship. That at any moment I think about who he is to me, my heart can't help but worship him.

We have to move away from making worship to God feel like a chore to it becoming our reasonable service. That it's not something we do begrudgingly but we worship because we are desperate for God. We have to get to a place in our mind that God's presence to us is our life support. When the life support is disconnected from us, we die. We have to become that dependent to God's presence. When God's presence becomes that to us, God will not have to call or beg us to worship him. Instead we will see it as a necessity to worship God. Lets pray together

"Father, thank You for working with us over these years. I know sometimes we are ungrateful and we loose sight of what is really important to us. Today we ask for Your forgiveness. We make a declaration we will forever be grateful for you being a good Father

towards us. On this day we change our attitude from feeling entitled to becoming grateful. Thank You Father for Your many blessings. Thank You for always being there for us. Thank You Father for never leaving us or forsaking us. Our lives are better because of You and we say thank You. Worship will no longer be a chore but our reasonable service towards You In Jesus Name we pray"

Amen.

Worship Reveals Your Heart

"The Lord says; these people come near to me with their mouth and honor me with their lips, but their hearts are far from me. Their worship of me is based on merely human rules they have been taught"-Isaiah 29:13

Have you ever seen yourself in a picture or video and thought wow, I look like that? I have fell victim to this as well. However, before we get up in the morning we plant ourselves in front of the mirror. We stay in the mirror so long that we convince ourselves how we believe we should look. We gloss over our imperfections and anything else that would lead us to feel bad about ourselves. We speak positives things to ourselves to make sure we can go out and win the day. Please don't get me wrong, there is nothing wrong with speaking positives thoughts; I do it myself. What happens when the positive things that we tell ourselves are really not positive thoughts at all? What happens when we make ourselves believe that we have no imperfections and everything about us is correct?

As individuals, we have a tendency to see all good and gloss over the bad. Consequently we are careful to bring out the bad or wrong we see in others. We are so intent on being better than others that we nit pick others just to make us feel good about ourselves. Which makes me pose a question to us all. What happens when we approach God in an intimate setting of worship and try to put on an act that we are perfect and we have it all together? When we believe that everything we give to God, He accepts? Please understand, worship has a way of revealing our hearts to us. There are no secrets we can hide from God.

When we enter into worship in an intimate way with God, He becomes the mirror we need to reveal our true reflection. Remember, we have a tendency to tell ourselves something for so long that we believe what we say. Even if what we are saying is hurting us more than helping. Remember, we can't hide our imperfections. We can't dress up enough or wear enough make up to cover our blemishes.

When we enter into the presence of God, it becomes extreme makeover. You've seen that show, Extreme makeover haven't you? The show is based on the premise of going to someone's home and the home being so bad, that they have to strip it down to the bear bones of the house. Sometimes the home is in such bad shape that they have to tear it down completely and start over. Well even though the people know there homes need fixing, when they come in they find stuff that they didn't even know lived in the home. Sometimes they find mold that is very bad to their health. Sometimes the foundation is so bad that people can't believe that the house is still standing.

When we enter into the presence of God, He becomes our home inspector. The bible tells us that we are Gods earthly vessels. We are the temples that houses

God's Glory. In other words, when we enter into the presence of God, we are automatically put through a home inspection. God goes through and shows you what we couldn't see about ourselves. Sometimes God finds things that are bad and toxic to our health. Things we wouldn't have seen if we didn't have someone to inspect it properly.

I believe what stops us from worshipping God, is we really don't want to see how we look. It's a mental boost for us to see imperfections in others but not ourselves. Often, we can't handle being shown we don't have it all together. Which causes us to never enter into the Holy of Holies. We praise God, shout, run or jump, but when its time for worship, we are tired. When worship starts, we wish it would move along quickly. Worship irritates us. I've seen people almost pass out running so hard, but when worship starts, they leave out of the sanctuary. To me, worship is the best part. Don't get me wrong, I love to praise God, but there is something about getting intimate with God that can't be compared to anything else. You began to become like David when he says, it's so good to get lost in his presence. God's presence breathes new life back into us. God's presence restores our strength. When I leave the presence of God, it's as if I received an oil change. I couldn't see it, but the old oil was causing me to become ineffective. I couldn't produce the way I needed to produce for God. I needed God to strip me of everything that was not like Him, so I could become better.

Sometimes we carry so much baggage and weight that we get used to it. Have you ever been on a trip and you had a lot of luggage? You went from your vehicle to your hotel to carry your things and grabbed everything you could. To you, you are just getting the job done carrying your bags. When you get close to the hotel and the bellhop ask you can he carry your bags, you breathe a sigh of relief once you release them. It is as if all the weight of the world was lifted off your shoulders. They are so helpful that you give them a tip for helping you.

Once we enter worship, God becomes our spiritual bellhop. He strips us from every heavy weight and baggage we have been carrying for so long. Since we have become complacent we have carried it for so long that it has become apart of us. We no longer pay the baggage any attention because we have gotten used to carrying it all of our lives. However, when God strips us of everything that is not like Him, our bodies breathe a sigh of relief. When those things happen, we can't help but to worship God. Our worship to God comes from our gratitude towards Him. The same way we show gratitude to the bellhop, in the form of a tip, for helping and relieving us of our baggage.

Do you realize how good of a father God is to us. Even in our tarnished state, God never stopped loving us. When we were broken, his love was strong enough to break all barriers, strip us down and rebuild us again. Why wouldn't we serve and worship a God like that? His love for us reveals that we are not worthy of the love He has given us. He should have cast us away, but His love drew us in. When our imperfections cause people to not want to be around us, God is waiting with His arms open wide. Why wouldn't we worship a Father like that? If our earthly father knew how to care and protect us daily, how much more do you think our heavenly Father can do? Don't you believe our heavenly Father will be better to us? ***Matthew 7:11 says "If you, then, though you are evil, know how to give good gifts to your children, how much more will your Father in heaven give good gifts to those who ask!"***

You see God is waiting on us to come into His presence. We do not have to be afraid of what we may see. Our worship to God reveals our hearts to help us become better. It's not to shame you, it is to show you that God loves us so much that imperfections do not scare Him off. God knows just what we need before we say a word. So why not allow God to remove our baggage, renew us, strengthen us and send us on our way? God is waiting on us today. I implore you to not leave Him waiting another day. Spend time with God and allow Him to show you the beauty of his Holiness. Let's pray together

"Father. First we want to say thank you. Thank you for seeing our imperfections and not turning Your back on us. Thank You for revealing our hearts to us. We want to say we are sorry for not spending time with you like we should. Today is a new day and we are coming to You to know You in a way we've never experienced before. Today, accept our worship and our sacrifice, because we want to know You beyond our thoughts or intellect. We love You Father. This is our prayer in Jesus's Name

Amen"

Worship Produces Love

"A new command I give you; Love one another. As I have loved you, so you must love on another"-John 13:34

As you look at what's going on in the world today, it can cause one to grieve how we treat each other. As each generation that comes along, the respect for each other leaves day by day. Social media has given people outlets to spew hatred towards people they may never get a chance to meet face to face. I've watched how young adults interact with each other and my heart hurts. There is no respect anymore. Most importantly, where is the love?

I can remember growing up and our parents making us show respect and love one another. It didn't matter if the people were family or not, they made us treat everyone as if they were family. We knew not to disrespect anyone, even if we weren't in front of our parents. We knew the repercussions that came with being disrespectful. Now a days, the parents are just as disrespectful as the children. We are seeing each generation being raised by another generation that was not taught how to love one another. As a result, this is a perpetual cycle that we must stop.

I started praying to God on different topics when this

topic was given to me, I had a perplexed look on my face. I wanted to know what does worship have to do with us loving one another. I asked God to please break this down to me because I wanted to make sure that I was doing my part of helping this generation, present, past and future.

God revealed to me as we worship Him, He shows us our shortcomings; how we do not have it all together. He revealed even with our shortcomings, His love for us never changes. He is still yearning for us to come dine with him in an intimate setting. God said in **John 13:24,** ***" I have given you all a command. I told you to love your neighbor as I have loved you***". I was amazed and I had to check myself. God didn't tell us love them under any type of condition or stipulation. He gave us a simple command. Love them because I loved you.

Now if God, being perfect in all his way, with no imperfections, can love us when He should frown upon us and turn His nose up at us; why can't we love one another? As I stated earlier, when we worship God, He reveals we don't have it the way we think.

We all have "skeletons" in our lives we wouldn't want anyone to see. Yes, we mask ourselves when we leave the safety of our homes. We appear to be in tiptop shape, but we are ugly on the inside. Our outer appearance doesn't line up with our inner appearance. We are what 2nd Timothy 3:5 describes as **"They will act religious, but will reject the power that make them Godly"**. Timothy ends the scripture by saying, **"Stay away from those types of people"**. If God, in all of His splendor and love, can love us past this situation, why can't we love each other?

What if you attempted to worship God and He turned you away because you aren't fulfilling His command He left behind? What if God treated us the way we treated others? Would we tell God that He is not being fair? Would we accuse God of having favorite people He loves to speak with? No, we would be describing ourselves. There is no way you can worship God and leave His presence and not show love to your neighbor. There is no way possible. If so, then you might want to check your worship. You might want to see if God really accepted your sacrifice. If He really heard you when you cried out to him.

Every time we worship, we leave a piece of our old self and begin to look like God. That's why in Genesis when Moses went to worship God and came back down the mountain the people were astonished.

God's glory had transformed Him. Are we being transformed when we leave God's presence? Are we staying in there long enough for the Glory of God to consume us, or are we only there just enough to say we worshipped? We should make a vow to ourselves that we will not leave the presence of God until we are changed. After we have finished worshipping God, our countenance and demeanor causes others to inquire about God.

Do we think we are a good representation of God when we treat others wrong? More importantly, when people interact with us, can they feel the love of Christ through us? When they leave us, would they be able to tell if we are God's children? Ask yourself these questions. Do we spend enough time with God so He can mold us into what He desires us to look like? Have we been telling the Potter what the clay should look like; or have we sat on the potter's wheel and declared to Him, make me into whatever You see fit.

That's what real worship does to us. It reveals our sinful flaws, even when we believe we have it all together. It allows God access to every room in our lives. It allows Him all access to our hearts. We come to Him ready to be changed. We realize that one encounter with God could be the difference in us making through our day, week or through life roller coaster.

True worship has a way of making even the toughest person bow in reverence of our Holy Father, King. God has a way of softening the hardest hearts through His worship. It's as if He performs a heart transplant on us. God takes away all of your past hurt and replaces it with his love. When we leave His presence, change has taken place. What we wouldn't do yesterday, we do today because we have a piece of him inside of us.

When we worship, Love is created within us and we give it to others like our Father did. This is what God is looking for on earth. Why aren't His children loving the way He loves? How can we expect change to take place if it doesn't first take place in us? Again, I present a question. Are we allowing God to purify our hearts and mold us into what He wants or are we telling Him that we are okay?

Do we see why God has need for us in the world beyond the four walls of the church? Can God trust us enough to impart His love in us, in order to give it away to others? Will we reserve it for certain people and not for all? There is no need for God to give us a heart transplant if we are going to damage it again. Let us make the decision to allow God to truly have his way with us. Allow God to change us and shape us into what he sees.

Please understand, when God sees us, he sees us as a finished product which he spoke into existence. Why not allow God to shape us when we worship. Let's all become agents of love to the world. Lets show the world everyday we love because God loves us. Unfortunately, some people will never get a chance to know God except through you. Let's allow God to transform us they way he did Moses in Genesis. Allow Him to make an impact and leave a lasting legacy on this generation, to love like Him. Lets pray together

"God, our precious Father. Thank You for allowing us to see ourselves like You. Thank You for loving us so much that You wouldn't leave us in the tarnished state

we are. We pray today You take full control of our lives and mold us into everything You see fit. Shape us into the loving vessel You are. You gave us a command to love our neighbors as You have loved us. Father, give us a heart transplant so we can love the way You love. Give us the ability to treat people with respect and love them past all of their hurt or failures. This we pray in Jesus name"

Amen.

When We Worship, We Allow God

To Amaze Us

"But it is written: Eye has not seen, nor ear heard, nor have entered into the heart of man the things which God has prepared for those who love Him. But God has revealed them to us through His Spirit. For the Spirit searches all things, yes, the deep things of God"-1 Corinthians 2:9-10

I love when I get to spend time with my wife. We live a hectic life, and when we get to spend quality time together, it's a great thing. One of our favorite things to do is to catch a good movie at the local cinema theater or snuggling on our couch with popcorn. We're amazed by something different every time we go. We prepare ourselves to get refreshments. As we go through the process of getting our tickets, our snacks, we walk towards the ticket master, present out tickets and we are off to see our movie. If you arrive early you can see commercials and information you may not know was in your town.

Then an awesome thing happens. While we are in a dark setting, alone with each other, even though the room can be filled to capacity, at that moment, nothing matters but my wife and our enjoyment watching a movie together. The previews start before the featured movie begins. The cinema normally shows four to five previews of new movies. A crazy thing happens. Before the movie starts to play, my attention is caught by one of the previews.

At that moment, my mind is blown. I went to see one thing and I left ready to see something entirely different. My interest was peaked to its maximum ability. It made me excited and anxious to come back to the movies. A crazy notion, even if the movie doesn't release until a few months away, I'm still excited. Every time we go to the movies thereafter, the preview is shown again and my interest level gets pushed through the roof once more. You may be wondering, why is this story relevant? God is the same way with us when we worship

Him.

Regardless if you are in the setting of your home or surrounded by your brothers and sisters in Christ in a church setting, He still has a way of amazing us. Every encounter we have with God, He always leaves us in awe. The bible tells us in ***John 4:24 that "God is Spirit and those who worship Him must worship in spirit and truth".*** We must worship in spirit and truth because with God being a spirit, His spirit gives us life and replenishes our spirit inside of us.

I love the way God treats us every time we enter into His presence. He always does something to amaze me. God has a way of showing us things, which cause us to love to have encounters with Him over and over again. When we enter in the spirit of God, we go in to worship Him and we leave in awe of something that He shows us.

The bible tells us in ***1 Corinthians 2:9-10 "But it is written: Eye has not seen, nor ear heard, nor have entered into the heart of man the things which God has prepared for those who love Him".*** What I found out is, we read that part and we get excited. I see preachers cite this scripture throughout services, but very rarely do I hear them go to the very next scripture. For those that take time to enter the presence of God and tap into the spirit of God, we are privileged to see the hidden things of God.

Even though we all love God, there are things that are withheld from us until we enter the presence of God. How do I know you might ask? We where just told ***"Eyes have not seen nor ear heard, nor have entered into the heart of man the things which God has prepared for those who love Him".*** But if you continue reading the bible, there is one caveat. Verse 10 says ***"But God has revealed them to us through His Spirit. For the Spirit searches all things, yes, the deep things of God".*** God has gifts our natural eyes and ears can't see or hear. However, God gives us clear instructions. He tells us, if you enter His presence and allow yourself to tap into His spirit, He will amaze us.

When my wife and I leave the movie theater, I always ask her what did she think of the movie. We go through our details of what we like or didn't like. Immediately following that discussion, we start discussing the previews we were privileged to see before the featured film. Our anticipation and excitement is through the roof over them. With the realization we know the coming attractions won't be released until months away, it doesn't diminish our excitement. Periodically, we find ourselves talking to each other about the preview we saw instead of the movie that we watched. God does us the same way.

The encounter we experience with God is awesome. The way He loves us when we tap into His loving spirit is indescribable. It's like nothing we have experienced before. Even though that experience was nothing like we have experience before, God has a way of revealing things to us, in His spirit, that leave us buzzing and salivating to get back into His presence.

Often, we try to explain to people what just happened and try to tell them what we have experienced but it doesn't do it justice. It seems there are no adjectives we can use to describe the grandeur of God that we experienced, and how amazing God is. He knows how to grab us, love us, reveal His deepest secrets to us and leave us in such amazement. It is hard for us to describe, or explain. Please tell me, why wouldn't we want to worship a God like that? Every time we leave His presence we are astonished. There are some things we are privileged to see that others are not privileged to see. Not because they can't, but they choose not to see it. Some things God will not reveal to us until we come into His presence.

Worshippers have a special place in God's heart. As we worship God, we pull on His heartstrings. We are not worshipping God to get something from God, but we worship God because He is our father. We worship Him because of our gratefulness towards Him. We find ourselves wanting to love God. When everyone else turned their backs on us and abandoned us because of our condition, God welcomed us with open arms. God knew how to take us in, clean us, equip us and empower us with everything we need to go through life and win. Why wouldn't we worship a God like that? Why wouldn't we set time aside from our busy lives to give reverence to the one, which allowed us to have the things we have?

When you worship God, those flash backs come to your mind all the time. You relive your past and see how God kept us over the years. You understand that God had his hands on us even when we weren't thinking about him. When death wanted us but God wouldn't allow it. When sickness wanted to take us but God healed our bodies. How the doctors were shocked at the results of the test when last time the prognosis was a couple weeks to live but now everything is healed. How your family was on the brink of splitting up and with surprise things got better rapidly. How your business was failing for a while and all of a sudden things turned around. How you had no idea how you would pass your final semester or exam but somehow things turned out better than you expected.

God has a way of Amazing us. Why wouldn't we worship a God like that? I just gave you a few examples of how our God has kept us over the years. I'm quite sure as you are reading this, you will begin to recall periods of your life when you didn't know how it would turn out; but in the end, YOU WON! Now, after all of that, God shouldn't have to beg or pull on us to worship him. Our life stories should cause us to bow down and worship him. The amazing thing is, as we continue to worship God, he will blow our minds again and again.

Today, make the decision to become a worshipper. Allow the love of God and the goodness of God to captivate your hearts. Go beyond the normal routine when we thank God. Go pass your normal experiences with God and cast yourself out into the deep things of God's presence.

Remember *1 Corinthians 2:10* tells us *"But God has revealed them to us through His Spirit. For the Spirit of searches all things, yes, the DEEP things of God'.* Let's move pass our surface relationship with God and cast our selves into the deep things of God. I guarantee that you will not drown in Him. God's been waiting to love on us. He is waiting to share things with us we can only receive when we enter into His spirit. Believe me, you will not be disappointed when you leave the presence of God.

In life, your spouse, family or friends, may have amazed you, but I guarantee you one thing, nothing compares when God amazes us. When God amazes us, it is breath taking. It's unlike anything we have ever experienced before. God's love surpasses anything we have felt in a lifetime. I love my wife and would die for my wife, but her love could never compare to the love of our Heavenly Father. My family may become angry with me and forsake me, but I have a promise from God He would never leave me or forsake me. Now I ask you this question one more time. Why wouldn't you worship a God like this? Lets pray together

"Father we love you. We come to you, not wanting anything from you, rather to tell you how awesome you are. Thank you for loving us when we deserved to be cast away. Thank you for allowing your Spirit to always lead and guide us always; if it was our decision, there is no telling how we would mess up our

lives. Thank you for allowing Your heart to be revealed to us as we worship You. How You show us Your secrets and leave us in awe. How Your presence takes our breath away and amazes us. Thank You for Your unfailing love You have for us. And because of Your love, we will never leave You. Even in our mistakes, we will always come running back to You. Life will never be the same without You, so today we vow to always long for You and yearn for Your Spirit. In Jesus's Name"

Amen.

I'm Determined To Worship and Live for God

"My Soul years, even faints, for the courts of the Lord. My heart and my flesh cry out for the Living God"-Psalm 84:2

From the beginning of this book until now, I pray you have read something that inspires you and pushes you to want to spend time with God. There are many things in life that can take up our time if we aren't careful. Our schedules can become overbooked if we let them. If you have a family, it's so important to prioritize our time. The children are usually in some extracurricular activities. Husband and wives are always busy with work and different projects. If your kids are still in school, homework has to be completed without counting a million other things happening with the family. If you are single, there are so many things to grab your attention. Many times when you are single, you are very career driven. You throw yourself into your work and it consumes you. Whether you are in school and it takes all your time throughout the day, you have to make sure you accomplish everything you intended to do.

If we are not careful, our day will be filled to capacity and we never leave space for God. I know I have been guilty of this myself. I wake up and get started right into my day. Before I know it, its night and time to rest for another day. If we are not careful, we begin to establish a routine that doesn't include God. We say we love God and He knows our heart. If you are in a relationship with someone and you never take time to talk or spend time with him or her, the other person will start to feel abandoned. It's not a healthy relationship when a person in the relationship is feeling unloved, unwanted or mistreated. Especially if you never take time to stop and say, "I love you" or "I miss you". The same way we have to keep the lines of communication open and fluid between our spouses, we have to keep them open with God.

We should never invest more time in other things than we invest in our relationship with God. I've learned the more time I spend with God, the easier it is to handle everything else. We become unhinged, cranky and may develop an attitude when our spouse deprive us of our quality time. It bothers us and we aren't ashamed or shy about letting them know our feelings. Well, how do you think God feels when we go minutes, hours, days, weeks, months or even years without spending time with Him?

The bible tells us in ***Exodus 34:14 "Do not worship any other God, for the Lord, whose name is Jealous, is a jealous God'.*** I know you would never worship another God over our Father, but do you understand, who or what you spend your time on or even think about more than God you put above God? Even though you say you love God, you aren't showing God your love through your actions. As it is in any relationship, you can say you love a person endlessly, but if there is no evidence of love, where is it? If there were never an action of love, how would one know that you love them? Love is not love until it is given away. That's what God is waiting on from us everyday.

God has always longed for us to spend time with Him. From the beginning of time when Adam was created, He walked in the garden hoping to spend time with Adam, but Adam hid himself from God. His sin and disobedience caused him to hide from God. God felt disappointment towards Adam because he had everything he ever needed or wanted but he wasn't satisfied enough to be in place when God appeared. When God appears to spend time with us, are we going to be in place? Are we ready to experience the goodness of God or are we too busy? Do we allow sin to keep us from experiencing the grandeur of God? There are many things that can keep us from God. It's our duty to prevent those things from distracting us from our alone time with God.

I am *determined* like never before to spend more

time with God. Regardless of my schedule, that's what I will do. I am prioritizing my life to insure God is at the center of everything that I do. I am determined to not allow God to feel as if He is second to anything. You have to become just like that. Accept, you will not allow God to feel second to your wife or husband, family, job, career, church, kids or anything. God has to always be the number one priority in our lives. When God is first, everything else falls in line. I'm not telling you that your life will be perfect and you will never have any challenges or obstacles to deal with. However, I will tell you if you have a healthy relationship with God, nothing is too hard for you to handle.

One thing that friends tease me about is that I'm blinded by my love of my wife. They joke and tell me when I'm with or around her or without her, they can tell that I'm thinking about her. Well, do you know your relationship with God should be even stronger than that? Do you know that your love for God should blind you to anything that would ever try to pull you away from God? God's love surpasses anything I can think of or imagine.

I am *determined*, today and forever more, that my worship to my Father will always be authentic. I'm *determined*, that my relationship with my Heavenly Father, will never go stale or stagnant. I'm *determined*, that my love for my God, will always cause me to make time for Him. I'm *determined* that my worship with my Heavenly Father, will always go deeper with every encounter I have with Him.

Today will you be Determined? Will you be Determined above everything that nothing will ever come between you and your Heavenly Father? If you have been reading this and you want to know God in this manner, you have the opportunity to know Him right now. ***Romans 10:9-10 say "That if you confess with your mouth the Lord Jesus and believe in your heart that God has raised Him from the dead, you will be saved. 10 For with the heart one believes unto righteousness and with the mouth confession is made unto salvation".***

It's just that simple. It's not a long drawn out process. You confess with your mouth and believe with your heart that our Lord and Savior Jesus Christ died for our sins; he was raised from the dead, YOU WILL BE SAVED. Salvation is free to everyone that confesses and believes on the Lord Jesus Christ.

If you want to rededicate your life back to God and start fresh, that's not a hard thing either. The bible tells us in ***Revelation 2:4-5 "Nevertheless I have this against*** *you, that you have left your first love. 5 Remember therefor from where you have fallen; repent and do the first works".* God says I have given you clear instructions on how to straighten your relationship out with me Revelation 2:4-5. It's again, that simple.

Foremost, I pray that this book has inspired you to examine your worship and relationship with our Heavenly Father. I pray this book has made you want to strengthen your relationship with our God. I pray this book has caused you to rededicate your life back to God. If you never knew God, I pray that this book gives you the desire to want to know Him. Lets pray together

"Lord God we come to You ready to strengthen our relationship with You. Some of us have never known you in our lives. Today we confess our sins to You. We ask You to forgive us of everything we have

ever done to disappoint You or hurt You. We ask You to come into our hearts and live with us forever more. Some of us want to rededicate our lives back to You. We left our first love and today we make the decision to return back to You. With your help God, we know we can face anything that life throws at us. Today Father, we say we love You. We thank You for many blessings upon our lives. We believe that nothing is to hard for You and we give ourselves over to You totally and freely. Freely we will worship You forever more. Freely we will live our lives unashamedly for You. Today starts a new day in You. Today we are healed from all past hurt or struggles. Today we are a new creation in Christ Jesus. Today we have resubmitted our love back to You. Today is the first day of the best day of our lives. Today we are SAVED and we are set FREE. Thank You Father for Your unfailing love towards us. We are

***DETERMINED TO WORSHIP YOU FOREVER.** In*

Jesus Name we pray

Amen!

NOTES

Craig A Morrisey

NOTES

Craig A Morrisey

ABOUT THE AUTHOR

Craig Morrisey was born in Warsaw, NC and now resides in Morehead City, NC. At a very young age, different Gifts and leadership were instilled in him. He spent his years growing and striving to cultivate his gifts, talents and relationship with God in order to help bless the world. He has always had a passion for people, helping them get closer to God for their purpose in life.

Craig has obtained a Bachelor's Degree in Theology and Associates in Biblical studies. He is the Minister of Music at Faith Tabernacle of Praise International Ministries, where he strives to relay the message that it is more important to have a relationship with God, than to try to perfect your gifts and talents. He travels to conduct various workshops and engagements to spread the message of growth in every area of people lives. It's his passion to see everyone mature in their relationship with God, themselves and ministry.

He is the husband of Crystal Morrisey, whom he loves, adores and has grown together for 12 years. He understands with God, family and ministry, there needs to be a balance in your life. If you keep God the center of attention throughout your life, your drive and focus can continue to grow and build a foundation that changes this world to a better place.

Reference

King James Bible

Merriam Webster Dictionary

New International Bible

Message Bible

New Living Translation Study Bible

www.ingramcontent.com/pod-product-compliance
Lightning Source LLC
Chambersburg PA
CBHW051946160426

43198CB00013B/2329